I0820838

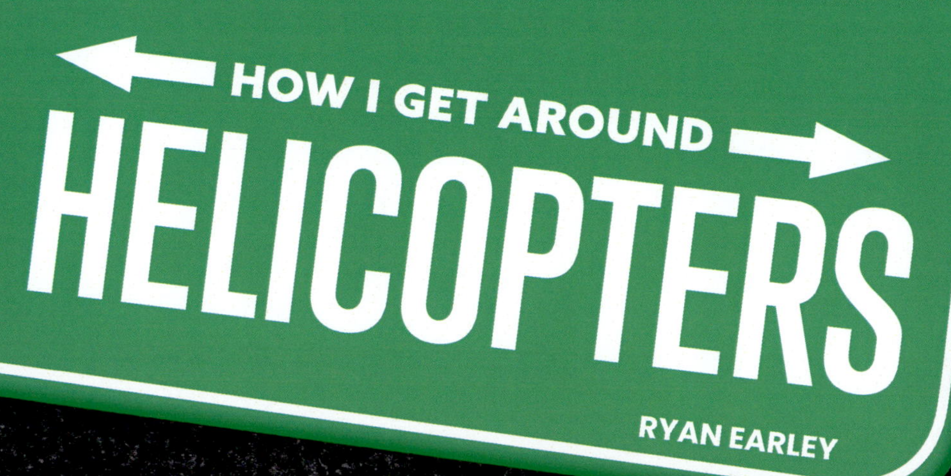

TABLE OF CONTENTS

A Pelican Book

Teaching Tips for Caregivers and Teachers:

Research shows that one of the best ways for students to learn a new topic is to read about it.

Before Reading

- Read the title and predict what the book will be about.
- Read the "Words to Know" and discuss the meaning of each word.
- Read the back cover to see what the book is about.

During Reading

- When a student gets to a word that is unknown, ask them to look at the rest of the sentence to find clues to help with the meaning of the unknown word.
- Motivate students with praise and encouragement.

After Reading

- Discuss the main idea of the book.
- Ask students to give one detail that they learned in the book.

Sight Words

all	four	in
around	get	many
by	have	the
fly	I	

Words to Know

blades

cockpits

engines

helicopter

landing skids

sky

I get around by **helicopter**.

helicopter

All helicopters have **engines.**

engine

blade

Many helicopters have four **blades**.

cockpit

All helicopters have **cockpits**.

All helicopters have **landing skids.**

landing skid

All helicopters fly in the **sky**.

sky
RF-13489

Index

Written by: Ryan Earley
Design by: Niko Magaro
Editor: Kim Thompson
Series Development: James Earley

Photos: All images from Shutterstock

Library of Congress PCN Data
Helicopters / Ryan Earley
How I Get Around
ISBN 979-8-8945-9260-2(hard cover)
ISBN 979-8-8945-9274-9(paperback)
ISBN 979-8-8945-9302-9(EPUB)
ISBN 979-8-8945-9288-6(eBook)
ISBN 979-8-8945-9316-6(audio)
ISBN 979-8-8945-9330-2(Read-Along)
Library of Congress Control Number: 2024946363

Printed in Canada/012025/CP20250101

Seahorse Publishing Company
seahorsepub.com

Published in the United States
Seahorse Publishing
PO Box 771325
Coral Springs, FL 33077